So...

IS HE GAY?

THE SINGLE WOMAN'S GUIDE TO WHETHER HE'D MAKE A BETTER GROOM OR CATERER AT YOUR WEDDING

● WRITTEN AND ILLUSTRATED BY LAURIE MITCHELL ●

LONGSTREET PRESS, INC.
Atlanta, Georgia

Published by LONGSTREET PRESS, INC.,
a subsidiary of Cox Newspapers,
a subsidiary of Cox Enterprises, Inc.
2140 Newmarket Parkway
Suite 118
Marietta, Georgia 30067

Printed in the United States of America

1st printing, 1996

Library of Congress Catalog Number 96-76501

ISBN: 1-56352-328-0

Book design by Neil Hollingsworth
Typesetting and production by Jill Dible

Dedication

To the reason for my happiness, my incomparable, category-defying husband Steve Jackman, who was hemming his curtains when I picked him up for our first date. Without his tireless assistance, advice, and support this book would truly not have been written.

Acknowledgments

I especially want to thank Leila Ganesan, who posed the original question, and Mike Kelly, for his tactful appraisal of the book's accuracy. For the generous enthusiasm, encouragement, and often unwitting examples offered by Kim, Clint, Rick, Ron, Marty, Mike, Lynn, John, Gary, Chuck, Mark, Pedro, Steve O., Jeff, Court, Chris, and Dave, I am extremely grateful. John Yow, Bethany Moreton, and the rest of the Longstreet Press staff managed to allay my fears and surpass my hopes for what the experience of publishing my first book would be. Lastly, a very sincere thank you to the life examples given by Bill, victim of, and victor over, hate, and to Bruce and Cliff, who entertain the angels.

CONTENTS

Foreword

What is a single woman, battle-fatigued by the uncertainties of the dating front, to do? Ask a man how many houseplants he has? Inquire how large his latest J. Crew order was? This book was written at the behest of a bewildered friend, who lamented that there ought to be a book detailing the many nuances indicating whether the targeted male is gay or straight. Now there is, but it's still up to you to determine whether he is a dork or not.

You know those old adages your mother used to offer as part of her cautionary tales about life? Such as, "Never judge a book by its cover," and "Appearances can be deceiving". Well, haven't you found other well-meaning advice to have little application to your adult life, like, "Boys won't care about the size of your chest; it's your bright personality and keen mind that they'll notice"? This absurd bromide should suggest not only that some preliminary conclusions may indeed be based on first impressions, but that in many cases a man's preference is so clearly stated by the way he chooses to look that wearing a sign would only be redundant.

	Gay	**Straight**
HAIR	Usually one of two basic styles: a. Errs on the side of brevity, as if quite proud of the shape of his skull. b. Cockatielish	Shortish, medium, or long, including the latter-day hippie look, the executive ponytail, and the "just so it's outta my eyes" functional.
HAIR MAINTENANCE	Standing appointments with stylist to whom he's slavishly devoted, named Elgin or Maurice.	Whoever's on duty at Mastercuts.
COLORING	Dyes hair to change color.	Dyes hair to cover gray.
FACIAL HAIR	Extremely short, trimmed with diamond-cutter precision.	Even if very short, probably longer than 1/8 inch.

Clothes

Gay |

	Gay	**Straight**
SHIRTS	Ironed. Never too tight anywhere. Find yourself admiring the pattern, colors, or texture; drawn to compliment him on his good taste.	Rumply. Only really take note if it's flannel.
JEANS	Perfect fit, clean, not frayed or patched. May also be ironed. (Special note: If jeans so tight you can tell how good a job the rabbi did, then he's seriously on the prowl, and won't be spending time with you, anyway.)	Possibly too tight around the waist from drying on high. Bottoms may be frayed from having bought too long— insists he's taller than he is. Worn spots from car keys, change, wallet.
SUITS	Each element a little out of the ordinary, such as purplish tint to the jacket, wide-wale corduroys, shirt discovered at butler uniform surplus shop.	Predictable navy suit, ensemble purchase, offset with a Bugs Bunny tie.

	Gay	Straight
SUITS (If rich)	More likely to buy a designer label. Armani is king.	More likely to go to a tailor.
JEAN SHORTS	Edges neatly turned back in 3/4-inch roll to reveal bronze, muscular thigh.	Legs of uneven length, fraying on own, hewed off with pocket knife.
TANK TOPS	Brightly colored, loose fitting, displaying a great body and perfect tan, especially when it's not particularly hot out.	Any shade including white, tight fitting, average body, mid-arm tan line. Only worn in 100°+ weather.

Accessories

	Gay	Straight
SOCKS, dress	Paisley, argyle, or some other striking, colorful pattern. As with shirts and rings, you'll find yourself admiring. Never droops around ankles. Never, ever, made of nylon.	Dark, thin, static-filled things you'd swear his grandfather had left him.

	Gay	**Straight**
SOCKS, casual	Thick, heavily textured gray socks with sharply contrasting orange or purple stripe, pushed down to one inch above lugger boots (see shoes, casual).	Bulky white tube socks he buys in bundles of a dozen.
SHOES, dress	Thin soles, coordinated with rest of outfit, in perfect condition.	Thick soles, comfort is foremost. Zealously insists that a favorite, dog-gnawed pair goes with everything.
SHOES, casual	Heavy, corrugated soles, half-height work boots in the 'junior lumberjack' style.	Severely beaten pair of whitish tennis shoes that he'll repair by holding any nylon parts over the gas range.
BELTS	Slim and understated, whatever works best with slacks.	Owns few, but inordinately attached to a weary, wide leather one that strains his current belt loops.

Gay	Straight

BELTS
(where worn)

Gay: Around the waist, no matter what his size.

Straight: Below the waist, ignores the sagging crotch, claims he wears the same size he did in high school.

HATS

Gay: Only worn now as part of a costume, such as Billy the Kid or a minor league batboy. The dreaded "hat hair" too high a price to pay for this accessory.

Straight: At some point a few years ago the John Deere cap merged with the baseball cap to give us the ubiquitous billed item that is stashed in the glove compartment, awaiting 5:05 PM Friday evening, when it becomes a symbiont to its host, the human head, where it remains until Monday morning. Just because Tom Selleck wore one for years on "Magnum, P.I.," other guys think they can too.

TIES

Gay: Real 1940s, hand-painted silk.

Straight: Retro '40s, printed.

	Gay	Straight
BANDANNAS	May be visible practically anywhere: loosely around the neck, tightly around the forehead or thigh, hanging from a back pocket. Never, ever, actually used for personal hygiene. That's what tissues are for.	Tucked out of sight in pocket, strictly for personal use. Will carry until it's crunchy.
BAGS	Won't happen. Anything resembling a purse shrieks of self-advertisement.	Only if from Europe or Latin America, will continue to carry less than two months once in USA.
GLASSES	New pair every six months, cutting edge of fashion. No aviator styles.	Wears pair bought from doctor until they break and tape will no longer hold together.
READING GLASSES	Wears on a cord or ribbon around his neck. Little crescent style preferred.	Refuses to get until 12 years after first needed, and you refuse to hold book and back away to focus for him.

Gay

Straight

FAVORITE COLORS TO WEAR

Gay: Aubergine, mauve, ecru, mocha, kiwi.

Straight: Brown, and the full brown family: beige, khaki, and tan. When asked, however, he'll say it's 'blue'.

Jewelry, if any

NECK

Gay: Usually a true pendant, a strictly aesthetic adornment. (Special note for the truly uninitiated: if he's wearing five interlocking, rainbow-colored rings, there is little more you need question.)

Straight: If a pendant, will probably be of a highly personal (i.e. religious) significance. Otherwise, a yellow gold, serpentine chain, the width a direct indication of the credit limit/desperation of the wearer.

FINGERS

Gay: Precise Zuni design in silver, or hand-cut malachite in gold, usually acquired "from a friend," on a fondly recalled trip, or knows the artist personally. As with his shirts (see above) you find yourself openly admiring their beauty and workmanship.

Straight: Huge, drawer-knob-sized class ring, or (yes, there are still a few out there) diamond pinkie ring.

	Gay	**Straight**
EARS	Small pierced earring in left ear.	Small pierced earring in left, or right, ear. Whatever.
WRISTS	One or more delicate, braided or knotted strips made of natural materials with a faintly tribal air. Watch for rainbow rings (see: Neck). If a loose-fitting gold chain is present, says, "I have money", or "I am loved by someone with money".	Gigantic metal watch; if cannot afford, may settle for gigantic metal chain or identification bracelet.

All men, both gay and straight, like to play dress-up once in a while. This should help you identify three of the more common poses assumed by both.

	Gay	**Straight**
COWBOY	All new apparel. No sweat stains around hatband. No matter how tight jeans are, can still slip a dime in the pocket, which no true cowboy could do. Hems not dragging on the floor by two inches; real cowboys gauge length of pants leg by how it looks when sitting on the horse.	Hat tilted back on head. Belt buckle smaller than a saucer. Jeans look like they might actually be comfortable to sit in.

GAY PRETEND COWBOY

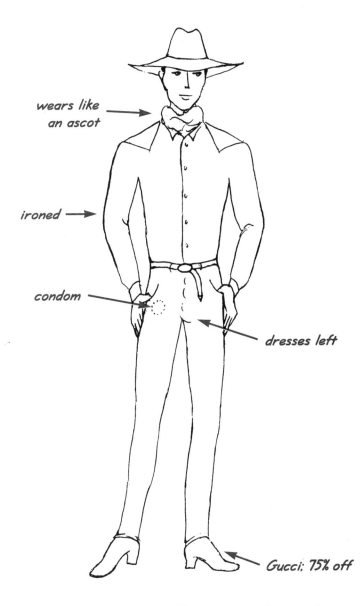

wears like
an ascot

ironed

condom

dresses left

Gucci; 75% off

Thinks he looks like J. Peterman catalogue ad

STRAIGHT PRETEND COWBOY

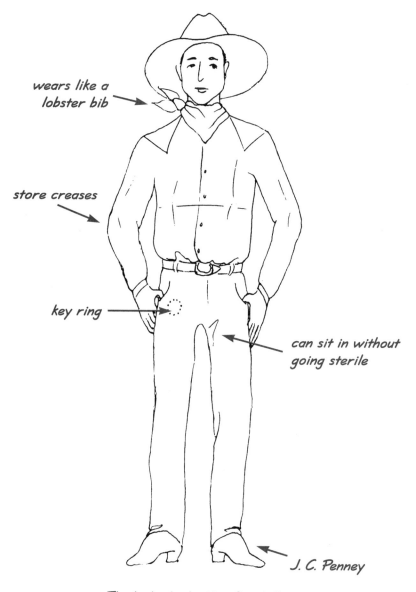

wears like a
lobster bib

store creases

key ring

can sit in without
going sterile

J. C. Penney

Thinks he looks like Garth Brooks

REAL COWBOY

wears &
uses

launders
monthly

Skoal

can't sit,
only leans

can't recall where
bought, or when.

Thinks he looks like Jesse James. Just might.

	Gay	*Straight*
PREPPIE	Clothing dry-cleaned, pressed; right brands but way too new, well cared-for. Creases in khakis, no scruff on top-siders. Looks as if he had a haircut within the last two weeks.	Clothing brand names out of date. Public schools, state college. No family money. Ill at ease. Name like Gus or Felix, not Jeff or Ted.
BIKER	Leather vest. Too trim, too fit. Only the most subtle, ambiguous of tattoos (e.g., a bracelet of orchids, rather than a bleeding rose with a knife through it). Landscape architect by day. Doesn't own a motorcycle. No hair sprouting from shoulders.	Leather jacket. Owns a motorcycle, used for "road trips with the guys," has less than 25,000 miles on it. Call themselves the "Weekend Warriors" or something like that. No tattoos. Accountant by day.
NAMES/nicknames exclusive to each	Unusual spellings, not ordained at birth, such as, Bill = Bil, Michael = Mycol, Rick = Ric or Rikk. Unexpected nicknames, as in, "My name is Alexander, but I go by 'Xan'".	Bubba, Hank, Boy, Junior, Alf.

HIS RESPONSE TO A RECEDING HAIRLINE

Straight

no one will
ever suspect

Mike Brady
poodle perm

carpet sample

gives up

Gay

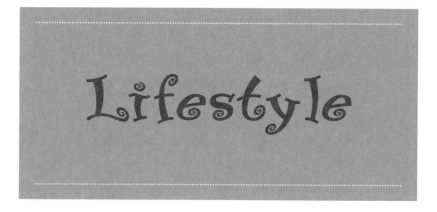

Lifestyle

Basically, this is getting to know him. What he has, what he does, where and how he does it, his habits and surroundings. Some of the things are on display for your appreciation; others will require your best detective skills honed from reading all those "Nancy Drew" books. Bet your mother never guessed how you would eventually use them.

	Gay	Straight
JOBS the other is less likely to be found as:	Antiques dealer, museum assistant, hotel desk clerk, travel agent, bookstore clerk, anything with theater or fashion in the description.	Engineer.

Education

	Gay	Straight
ELEMENTARY	Teased for requesting a moist towelette after fingerpainting.	Popular for making the best fake boogers with his Elmers glue.
HIGH SCHOOL	Really proud of his role as Mercutio. Asked specifically for the part.	Really proud of his "scores." Try to change the subject.
TRADE	Nursing school	Trucking school
B.A.	Psychology, with no intention to use professionally	Physical Education

	Gay	**Straight**
THE ARTS, although he's more smart than talented	Art History (hopes to be a critic)	Architecture (butch art, read Ayn Rand)
BUSINESS	Personnel	Finance
RELIGION, but only if he is an enthusiastic practitioner. If the subject comes up only when he's filling out a hospital entrance form, don't consider it a criterion.	Convert to Catholic, Episcopalian, Orthodox, or Jewish, in order to satisfy need for ritual, tradition, and pageantry.	Southern Baptist or Mormon. (Even if he is gay, is so deeply repressed he wouldn't know it.)

His House or Apartment

HE HOPES YOU'LL ADMIRE HIS...	color scheme.	apparent importance as illustrated by the distribution of at least two telephones per room.
DREAM HOME	Victorian mansion	Log cabin
SIGNIFICANT FEATURE WHEN SELECTING	Light and space	Number of outlets

	Gay	Straight
JUDGES AN APARTMENT COMPLEX	on approach	once inside
NEIGHBORHOOD	Interested in the "look."	Interested in the distance to work.
IF HAS A HOUSE	1930s or earlier. Beautifully renovated, or in the process of leading the neighborhood in gentrification. Nothing like the house he grew up in.	A lot like the house he grew up in. 1950s or later suburban tri-level. Pretty good at keeping the lawn mowed.
IF HAS AN APARTMENT	Either a small grouping of brick buildings with a courtyard, or a century-old mansion converted into a few individual flats.	Huge, multiplex compound, units numbered with up to four digits. Mandatory pool and clubhouse that he never uses.
WALLS	Mauve, sand, apricot, taupe, or blush.	Whatever color they were when he moved in.
FLOORS	Polished hardwood floors with several colorful, handwoven American Primitive rag rugs.	Wall-to-wall dark brown, deep pile polyester carpet.

HIS NEW SURROUNDINGS NEED IMPROVEMENT

BEFORE

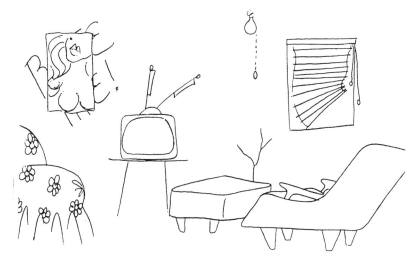

TWO WEEKS LATER

Straight

BEFORE

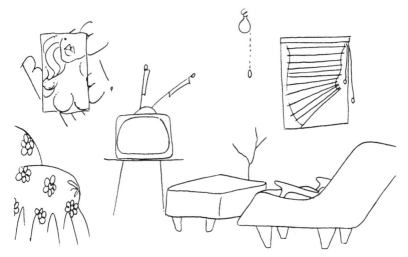

SIX MONTHS LATER

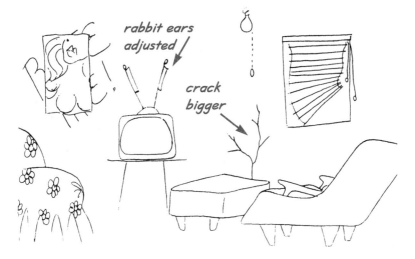

rabbit ears
adjusted

crack
bigger

	Gay	*Straight*
CLAIMING IT AS HIS OWN	Will arrange, paint, refinish, sacrifice for a total look. Appearance valued over comfort.	Comfort valued well over appearance. Puts up whatever he likes, as long as he likes it.
HOME IMPROVEMENT GURU	Jocasta Innes	Bob Vila
ON WALLS	30 to 80 perfectly matted and framed photographs, etchings, and watercolors of a purely decorative nature.	Rock concert posters, push-pinned directly into the wall.
LIVING ROOM	Antique chairs reupholstered in a rich brocade, charming loveseat, floor lamps.	Six-foot long sagging couch, sleeps on it more than on bed. Remote control and TV Guide on floor in front of couch. Two lawn chairs set up if he's expecting company.

	Gay	Straight
EVIDENCE OF ELECTRONIC ENTERTAINMENT	Handsome vintage radio, doesn't work; sleek CD player.	Massive, expensive, state-of-the-art multimedia system that resembles a wall from NORAD; took three evenings just to program the doormat-sized remote control.
KNICK-KNACKS	In abundance. Souvenirs from trips, gifts from friends, vases, bits of porcelain, figurines of a favored animal like a pig, dotting most flat surfaces. Not a speck of dust. Watch for any sign of a doily.	Few in evidence. What little on display often has great personal significance to him, like a Rubix cube he's been trying to solve for 11 years, or a coiled, laminated rattlesnake ashtray.
MAGAZINES	Interview, Details, GQ, Vanity Fair, Movieline	Time, Money, Sports Illustrated, Byte, Popular Mechanics
CATALOGUES	Williams Sonoma, International Male, Spiegel	J.C. Whitney, Pro Bass Shop, Victoria's Secret

HOME IMPROVEMENT PROJECT

Gay

Straight

	Gay	**Straight**
SPORTS EQUIPMENT	Beautiful antique wicker creel – he doesn't fish. Lovely embroidered St. Andrews hand towels – he doesn't golf.	Disgusting old coffee can for worms – he actually fishes. Horrifying pants and unpleasant shoes – he actually golfs.
DINING AREA	Antique cherry wood dining table, eight matching chairs, four leaves.	TV trays.
WINDOWS	Swags of peach-colored woven ramie, knotted to one side.	Vinyl off-white shades.
BREAKFAST NOOK	Actually in use as a breakfast nook. Predominantly yellow, with a '50s chrome and vinyl dinette set.	Storage space for over-sized microwave on obsolete LP cart. Only appliance used in kitchen.

Gay

Straight

	Gay	**Straight**
KITCHEN	Superbly stocked pantry and refrigerator, down to the homemade raspberry vinaigrette. Herbs and spices alphabetized. Garlic and chili pepper braids suspended from ceiling. Lots of vitamins. Impressive collection of appliances like bread machine and food processor that he uses regularly. Complete set of Fiesta, Harlequin, or Lu-Ray dishes.	Shelves stocked mainly with mixes with 'helper' in the title. Stove turned on only for grilled cheese sandwiches. Nothing baked. Refrigerator contains 46 itty-bitty drive-thru condiment packets, two eggs, carton of milk, leftover pizza, coke, beer, film, and batteries. Bare countertop except for a giant jar of peanut butter, loaf of bread, and a Mr. Coffee. Owns two plates, nine forks, 37 plastic stadium glasses.
REFRIGERATOR ITSELF	A colorful variety of magnets festooning the surface, holding up snapshots of friends, nieces and nephews, postcards from sunny destinations, pet's medication schedule and vet's number.	Door slightly sagging on hinges, will no longer seal properly from hanging open for extended periods while owner ruminates on contents and scratches self.

HIS SHELVES

Gay

"stole" at auction while friend distracted competing bidder

photos of self with cooperative celebrities

in case friends drop by

feeds with eyedropper. constantly repotting

never, ever uses

TUSCAN VILLAS
MICHELANGELO
TIFFANY GLASS
SAUCES

treasured autograph

really a lighter—he smokes, but would never dream of using it

thinks it's "a scream"

plays to show off his attributes

knows every word of every song on CDs, and will prove it with very little prompting

Celebrity Trivia

TWISTER

Straight

has moved shelves
14 times since
freshman dorm

keeps trophies up
high so the "most
improved player"
not visible

in case
friends
drop by

plant dead for
2 years—keeps
forgetting to
throw out

anything
found on
floor

WSU WSU WS

treasured
autograph

really a lighter—
doesn't smoke,
but plays with it
constantly.

actually
likes

CLANCY
CLANCY
CLANCY
CLANCY
THE FIRM

plays
for
blood

BATTLESHIP
RISK

CDs obsessively organized.
can find REM's "Monster"
in the dark.

	Gay	**Straight**
CAN UNDER SINK	Glade	Raid
BEDROOM	Four-poster bed with antique quilt, found at auction, rescued from grandmother's attic, or made himself. Laundry in a hamper.	King-sized water bed, black vinyl bumper pads, fake fur cover. Refers to as "the playing field." Laundry in the corner.
READING MATERIAL ON NIGHTSTAND	Ol' Possum's Book of Practical Cats	The Art of War

Don't Overlook the Little Things

	Gay	**Straight**
USES TWEEZERS TO	avoid the ear-to-ear Neanderthal brow	remove splinters from gouging dugout canoe
USES A MALLET TO	flatten chicken breasts	pound tent stakes
SHEARS ARE FOR TRIMMING	piecrusts and candlewicks.	toenails and ear hair.
TOOTHPICKS ARE	for holding rumaki together, and skewering the olive.	stiff floss.

	Gay	**Straight**
FAVORITE G.I. JOE	Sailor. Still has, displays, and plays with.	Green Beret. Won't admit he still has, and plays with.
FAVORITE DOLL	Barbie—Donna Karan or Bob Mackie	Inflatable
FAVORITE TOOL	Lemon zester	Swiss army knife
OVERALL IMPRESSION	In addition to the preponderance of either art deco or movie memorabilia, it's the attention to details, as in the careful selection of stamps, coasters, shade of toilet paper, etc.	Whatever works, fits, cost less, or was jettisoned from his mother's house when she redecorated.

Pets

	Gay	**Straight**
DOGS	Small, cute dogs. If large, should be a stunning, sleek purebred like a Dalmatian or a Borzoi.	Large dogs, as if he may need to hunt or defend his home at any moment. Looks don't matter; battle-scarring often adds to appeal.

HIS PETS

Gay

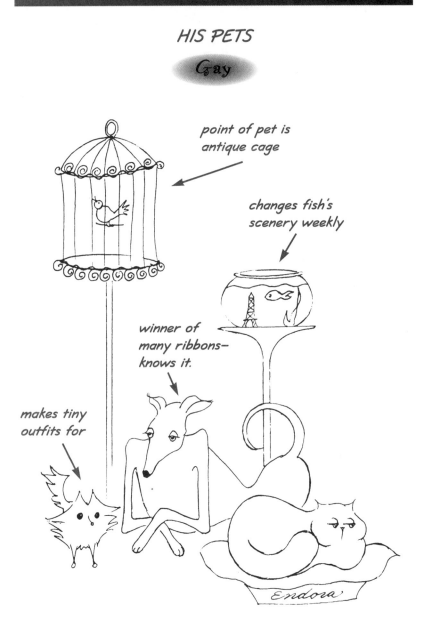

point of pet is antique cage

changes fish's scenery weekly

winner of many ribbons— knows it.

makes tiny outfits for

Endora

Straight

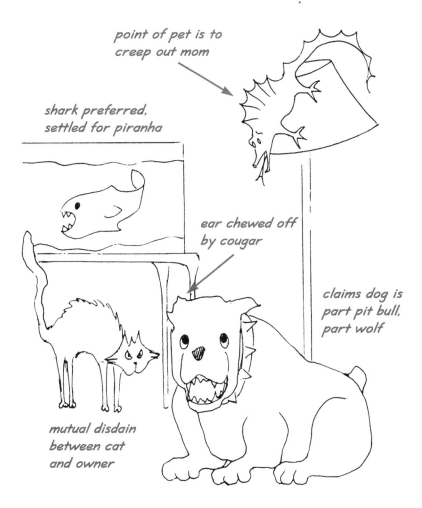

point of pet is to creep out mom

shark preferred, settled for piranha

ear chewed off by cougar

claims dog is part pit bull, part wolf

mutual disdain between cat and owner

	Gay	
DOG NAMES	Dorian Grey, Frodo, Fanny, Aloysius	Bruno, Caesar, Ruffian, King
CATS	Gorgeous, pampered; coats are especially beautiful from constant brushing.	Cat fed.
CAT NAMES	Audrey, Marlene, Pussy Galore, Barbra, Kitty Carlisle	"Cat"

Home Maintenance

CLEANING	Knows what and where the lintel is, and keeps it spotless, along with everything else.	Removes underpants from kitchen counter before company comes.
SOMETHING OUTSIDE NEEDS PRUNING. HE GETS THE	pruning shears.	chain saw.
LAUNDRY	Fourteen color piles. Subdivide into dry clean, pre-soak, hand wash, and those items too delicate for any cleansing, must destroy after one wearing.	Waits until down to last pair of gym shorts. Finally hauls one duffel bag full of whites, two pillow cases of non-whites to the laundromat.

Gay

Straight

TAKES TRASH OUT

Gay: 4-8 times per day. Uses small white plastic bags with twist ties, about the size of lunch sacks.

Straight: once a week, if then. Engineering feat to see how much can cram into single, overflowing trash can, then test of balance and strength to carry out in one trip. Grumbles about doing, but secretly gives him a great sense of accomplishment.

WHILE WORKING OUTSIDE, HE GETS THIRSTY. HE

Gay: removes gloves, wipes feet, goes inside, takes chilled Naya from refrigerator, pours into French bistro glass, adds mint leaves from window box, ice, twist of lime.

Straight: turns on hose.

USAGE AND WASTE

Gay: Recycles all disposables, but will take an unflattering item of clothing to the Junior League Thrift after wearing once.

Straight: May recycle crushed aluminum cans, if he thinks about it. However, will wear jeans until his wallet completely wears through the pocket.

SOMETHING NEEDS REPAIRING. HE REACHES FOR

Gay

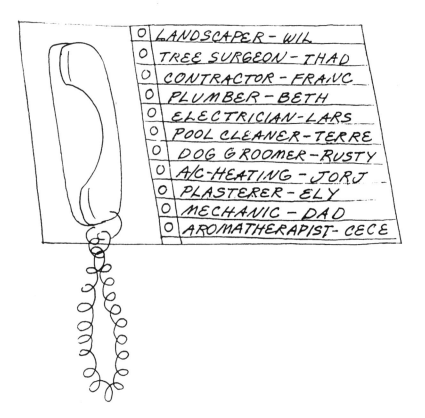

O	LANDSCAPER - WIL
O	TREE SURGEON - THAD
O	CONTRACTOR - FRANC
O	PLUMBER - BETH
O	ELECTRICIAN - LARS
O	POOL CLEANER - TERRE
O	DOG GROOMER - RUSTY
O	A/C-HEATING - JORJ
O	PLASTERER - ELY
O	MECHANIC - DAD
O	AROMATHERAPIST - CECE

Straight

Toiletries

 Gay  **Straight**

	Gay	Straight
SOAP	Honey Oatmeal Scrub	Safeguard
DEODORANT	Eucalyptus and Tea Tree Oil	Right Guard
SHAVING CREAM	Mostly Men Facial Gel for Sensitive Skin	Shield (Note defensive theme at work in selections)
EXFOLIATOR	Loofah	Washcloth
SHAMPOO	Body Shop's Grapefruit Frequent Wash	Head & Shoulders (even if he doesn't need it)
COLOGNE	Citrusy	Woodsy

Exercise

Gay   **Straight**

	Gay	Straight
PURPOSE	Exercises to stay slim	Exercises to stay fit
CONSIDERS HIMSELF FAT WHEN HE CAN	pinch a centimeter	no longer see his feet, the footstool, or the bottom half of the TV screen.
CONSIDERS <u>YOU</u> FAT WHEN	your butt finally blows out the stitches of your Chanel suit.	you retain 4 ounces of water.
WEIGHTS	Lifts weights to gain muscle and definition	Lifts weights to gain size and strength
CARDIOVASCULAR FITNESS	Aerobics class	Running
AFTER A WORKOUT	Glowing forehead	Underarm rings
PROOF OF STRENGTH	Holding both your shopping bags and his while you look for your key.	Crushing beer cans against his forehead.

HE RETURNS FROM A TRIP TO HAWAII WITH

Travel / Shopping

Gay   **Straight**

	Gay	Straight
PREFERRED CLIMATE	Hot	Cold
PREFERRED TERRAIN	Beach	Mountains
DESTINATIONS	Mediterranean cruise, Provincetown, Tuscany, Paris, Key West	Camping
ACCOMMODATIONS	Bed and Breakfast	Tent
ADVANCE PLANNING	Sends for brochures months ahead. Calls travel agent, with whom he is on a first-name basis. Tells agent exactly where wants to go, the area of the beach, the view from the room, low-fat cream cheese on the morning breakfast tray.	None. Prefers lengthy driving trips, no reservations. Assumes there will be a vacancy, KOA, rest stop, or wide spot to pull over when he finally gives in after 19 straight hours of driving.

	Gay	**Straight**
PACKING	Starts one week ahead. Three to four outfits per day. This is the time to have fun, and a great excuse to enhance wardrobe. Matched, soft-sided luggage, either nubby tapestry or many-buckled leather. Adds sombrero at last minute, as one never knows when a costume party may break out.	Starts 45 minutes before trip begins. Packs two cleanish shirts, one pair white socks, three pairs of underwear, and an extra pair of jeans, just in case. As an afterthought, adds toothbrush. Can pack entire contents for two week trip in one gym bag. You bring the deodorant and razor.
WHILE BROWSING IN A FOREIGN OPEN-AIR MARKET, YOU GET SEPARATED. YOU FIND HIM	pricing and comparing baskets that will be used strictly for adornment in his kitchen.	watching the tattooed woman wrestle the cobra.
POSTCARDS	Writes 15-30 chatty postcards his second day there. Usually features some small, decorative detail, is a campy throwback, or will embarrass your mailman.	You've got to be kidding.

	Gay	Straight
PHOTOGRAPHIC RECORD OF TRIP	Lots of little pictures of the bus driver, an appealing cornice, every single place where food, drinks, or souvenirs purchased, some interesting tilework he'd like to find for the kitchen. Main difference: loves to have someone in every picture, most often the person he's travelling with.	A few carefully selected shots capturing the famous landmark, edifice, or vista as it has never been photographed before. Expensive cameras, lenses, tripods. Won't take pictures of others since he hates to have his own taken, and doesn't see the point of photographing his travelling companion. Learn to stand so as not to cast shadows on his subject.
UPON RETURNING, SOMEONE ASKS, "HOW WAS YOUR TRIP?"	"Very 'Madwoman of Chaillot'" or "Very 'Through the Looking Glass'" or "Just like 'Brigadoon!'"	"Made 720 miles in 9 hours, 22 minutes. Only one ticket from that SOB at the state line I didn't deserve."

	Gay	Straight
SHOPPING (should have appeared under 'maintenance' for straight description)	Seven hours, or until *you're* exhausted. Has every designer bargain staked out. He's just certain the Mojave cable knit at Saks will perfectly complement the persimmon twill slacks at Macy's. He's right. It does. Then he starts picking out *your* clothes.	Fourteen minutes. Complains, wants to sit, eat, or just go. Finally appeased with one-hour visit to the electronics department.
FLOWERS HE'LL SELECT FOR YOU	Birds of Paradise, Calalily (Lily Munster or Morticia Addams fan), or orchid—will spend 20 minutes telling you how to care for it.	Roses, when prompted. Red: you've got a ring. All other colors: you don't have a ring.
SHOPPING FOR GREETING CARDS	Can languish for hours in card shop. Must read every one before making a decision; once perfect one found, has picked out nine more, often with no particular recipient in mind.	Usually needs to be reminded by family member or you that a card is needed. Waits until he's driving to the party to purchase, grabs biggest, fuzziest one and signs in car.

Food

	Gay	Straight
FAST FOOD	Vegetarian sandwich with alfalfa sprouts on 7-grain bread, sushi.	Cheeseburgers
FOOD TO EAT IN CAR	None. Too easy to spill, and nothing gets out mustard.	Beef jerky
FOOD TO IMPRESS YOU	Vichyssoise, nasturtium salad, duckling morello, asparagus with capers, crème brulée.	Great big steaks
BARBECUE	Skinless, boneless breasts of chicken. Beef considered only as a shish kebab ingredient.	Beef
REAL POINT OF BARBECUE	The marinade	The fire
MEALS	Brunch, late afternoon tea, midnight buffet.	Breakfast, lunch, dinner.

HE SUGGESTS HAVING LUNCH OUTDOORS

Gay

he brings

chooses view

Straight

he brings

chooses view

Gay | Straight

EATING OUT

Gay

Sits facing mirror. Ought to be a plant somewhere. May go in for demi-grunge, that is, pretends he's slumming in a diner mock-up or an ethnic 'dive' one block off of the chi-chi area. Has a few regular spots, but loves to try new places. Charming with female server, appraising if male server younger and cuter than he is. Orders dessert. Tips in strict 15-20% range.

Straight

Sits with back to wall, one eye on the door. Judges restaurant by the meat entrée and size of portions. Has two or three favorites for best ribs, best T-bones, etc. Goes in for true grunge, the real health department targets. Flirts with female server, edgy and critical with younger, cuter male server. Doesn't order dessert. Tips too much or too little.

HE SAYS: "CAN I GET YOU SOMETHING TO DRINK?"
YOU SAY: "THANK YOU. SOME TEA WOULD BE NICE."

FIVE MINUTES LATER, HE BRINGS IN:

Straight.

Beverages

	Gay	**Straight**
SOFT DRINKS	Snapple, NY Seltzer, Diet Fresca.	Coke, Pepsi, Dr. Pepper, Root Beer.
BEER	Zima, O'Douls, non-Coors beer.	Beer
WINE	Christian Brothers, wine coolers.	Prefers red, may try white with fish, can't bring himself to order rosé.
MILK	Only to pour over all-natural granola, add to omelets, or the occasional bechamel sauce.	Drinks straight from carton.
KNOWS MILK HAS GONE BAD	Three days before expiration date—you can't be too careful	Moss on north side of carton

Activities

	Gay	Straight
DANCING	He's better than you are.	If he'll dance at all, thinks it's ok to dance like John Travolta since he's popular again.
SOMEONE SHOUTS, "Let's do the Hokey-Pokey!"	He's the one that shouted, "Let's do the Hokey-Pokey!	Considers hitting whoever shouted, "Let's do the Hokey-Pokey!"
HOBBIES	Gourmet cooking, Reupholstering antique furniture, container gardening, dusting and re-arranging his knick-knacks.	Washing, waxing, repairing, driving his car, ham radio, shooting animals, sleeping, golf.
SINGS	in community choir.	in the shower.

	Gay	**Straight**
TALENT	Determining within 5% the poly/cotton ratio of any fabric at touch.	Catching insects in mid-air with his bare hands.
EVENING CLASSES	Ballroom Dance, Northern Italian Cooking, Rug making, Wine tasting.	Pyramid Sales Schemes That Cannot Fail! Wealth Through Legal-ized Sports Betting!
INDOOR GAMES	Charades	Strip poker
OUTDOOR GAMES	Croquet	Lawn darts
MORE LIKELY TO PLAY	Volleyball	Softball
FAVORITE AMUSEMENT PARK RIDE	Ferris wheel. (You both take advantage of repeat opportunities to view the operator.)	Death-ride 9000. (Only pretends to enjoy it. Is actually scared stupid throughout ordeal.)

HIS ANTIQUES / COLLECTIBLES

Gay

(intentional)

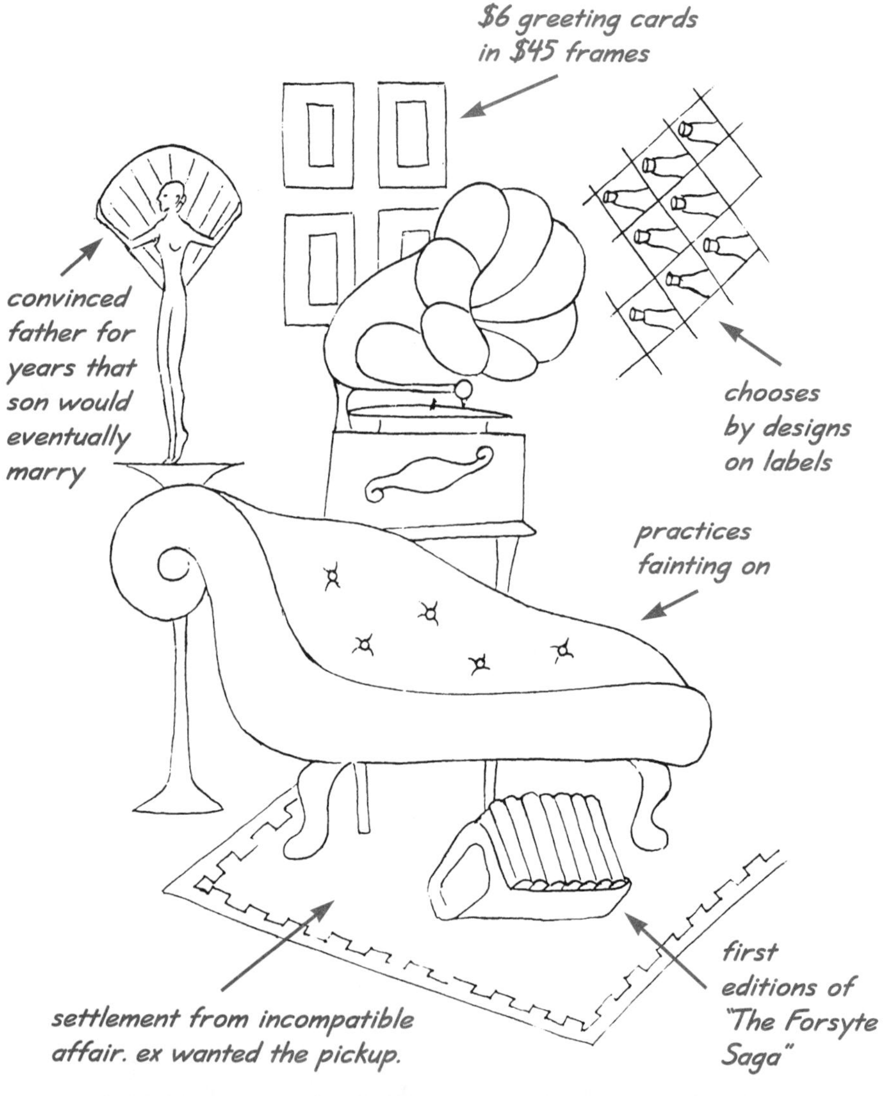

$6 greeting cards
in $45 frames

convinced
father for
years that
son would
eventually
marry

chooses
by designs
on labels

practices
fainting on

settlement from incompatible
affair. ex wanted the pickup.

first
editions of
"The Forsyte
Saga"

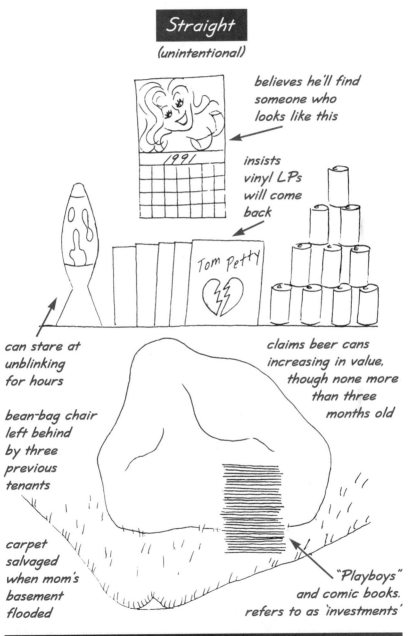

Straight

(unintentional)

believes he'll find someone who looks like this

insists vinyl LPs will come back

can stare at unblinking for hours

claims beer cans increasing in value, though none more than three months old

bean-bag chair left behind by three previous tenants

carpet salvaged when mom's basement flooded

"Playboys" and comic books. refers to as 'investments'

	Gay	**Straight**
SIDE-SHOW ATTRACTION	Alfred/Alfreda, The Amazing Half-Man/Half-Woman. He makes whispered comments about depilatories and Scotch tape throughout the act.	Serpentina, the female contortionist, who can purportedly peel a banana without the use of her hands, feet, or mouth. Refuse to let him go.
VOLUNTEERS	to help you find a dress for dinner at your boss's house.	to help you move, as long as it's not in with him.
RAINY AFTERNOONS	Textiles exhibit at the art museum	Sport, boat, and travel show.
SNOWY DAYS	Makes a Botero-esque female figure, accessorizes with plastic purse and pill-box hat.	'Writes' his name.
SPECIAL OCCASION PARTIES, AS GUEST	Goes to every wedding, bar mitzvah, and shower he's invited to. Selects an elegant, marginally useful gift, e.g., a crystal baby bottle.	Goes only when dragged or threatened. Mother, sister, or you selects and buys the gift.

	Gay	**Straight**
GIFT WRAPPING	Handmade paper, fleur-de-lis pattern stamped in gold leaf, cloth bow, real holly berries and pine needles.	Store sack with receipt and price still on (easier to return), or done by his adoring neighbor whose unrequited love for him makes her do any humiliating thing he asks
YOU INVITE HIM TO A PARTY. HE ASKS	"What can I bring? I have a great recipe for paella."	"Is it a kegger or BYOB?"
YOU GIVE DIRECTIONS TO THE APARTMENT COMPLEX	"Oh the one that recently painted the eaves sienna and replaced the rock garden with jonquils?"	"Yeah, I once got drunk at a frat party there and dove into the pool while it was empty."
SHOWING UP	Arrives early, brings flowers, helps host by mincing shallots.	Arrives late, empty-handed, asks where the beer is.
CONTRIBUTION TO A POT-LUCK DINNER	Layered casserole with sculpted puff pastry top. Stayed up late the previous night fixing, but swears it was no trouble. Needs 10 minutes more at 350°.	2-liter bottle of Coke that he got free with fill-up at the corner gas station.

HE IS INVITED TO A COSTUME PARTY

Gay

assumes his wit sufficient to portray Noel Coward. It isn't.

if he sings, "Stop, in the Name of Love" one more time, you'll kill him.

Tallulah Bankhead— really his Bette Davis with a Southern accent

seems to know where to find size 12 pumps.

Straight

conceptual artist,
and a lamp—no
one will talk to.

thinks this is a
costume—sadly,
also thinks it's
funny.

custom-made
ears, suit has been
let out several
times. RUN.

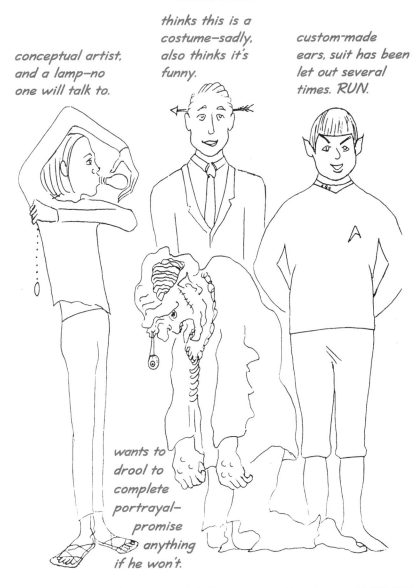

wants to
drool to
complete
portrayal—
promise
anything
if he won't.

Day of His Party

	Gay	Straight
REASON FOR PARTY	Watch Miss America Pageant, chat	Watch the game, drink
6:30 AM	Up, stretching	Asleep
6:45-7 AM	Shower, grooming	Asleep
7-7:15 AM	Light breakfast of hazelnut roast decaf and 23-grain muffin.	Asleep
7:15-8 AM	Study Martha Stewart's Entertaining	Asleep
8-9 AM	One hour call _to_ mother. Chats about her shoulder surgery, thanks her for the box of knitted place-mats.	Call _from_ mother wakes him. Pretends he wasn't asleep; she responds that he couldn't sleep that late if he had chil-dren. Call lasts 10 minutes. Spends remaining 50 minutes in bathroom reading the newspaper.

	Gay	**Straight**
9-9:10 AM	Feed Cleocatra from tiny, individual foil pouch.	Feed Thor from 50-pound bag
9:10-10 AM	Play Cindy Crawford workout video and actually work out. Showers again.	Play Claudia Schiffer workout video, watch while laying on couch eating a black banana and leftover burrito.
10 AM-Noon	Makes checklist out: purchase swizzle sticks shaped like scepters, errands to be run, etc. Arranges chairs for best viewing. Adds leaves to table. Irons Caribbean motif tablecloth. Polishes drinking glasses and adds ribbon sashes with Miss (state of origin) to identify person using.	Nap.
Noon-1 PM	Takes time for quick but healthy lunch with seven close friends at "The Ambivalent Bagel."	Scratching, yawning. Checks refrigerator for more leftovers, reheats some Little Caesar's breadsticks. Considers showering.

	Gay	*Straight*
1-4:00 PM	Visits the gourmet specialty store, the bakery, the coffee importer, the wine merchant, the party supply store, the kosher butcher, the flower shop, the kitchen appliance boutique, the garden supply store, and the video rental—just in case.	Back on couch. Golf Classic on TV, but channel surfing constantly. Catch up on back issues of Sail (doesn't own a boat, doesn't live near water). Thinks of calling girl who dumped him last year, decides not hearing from him would be greater punishment.
4-4:30 PM INVITATIONS	Back home. Goes over list of those who RSVPed his written invitations mailed 18 days prior.	Remembers he ought to call the people he wanted to have at party. Calls them, all can come.
4:30-5 PM LAST MINUTE PURCHASES	Realizes he forgot the surprise party gift. Dashes out to "The Neon Bustier."	Runs to local convenience store. Buys beer, ice, snacks, pop.

	Gay	**Straight**
5-5:30 PM CLEANING	A little light hoovering. (Since he spent Wednesday through Friday evenings sterilizing an already immaculate house, this is all the cleaning necessary.)	Shoves unfinished magazines and newspapers behind door. Shoes under couch, socks under couch cushions. Dirty dishes in dish washer—too many—remainder packed in microwave. Sweatsuit he wore all day tossed in oven. Flushes toilet.
5:30-5:45 PM DECORATIONS	Game of Monopoly on display in honor of Atlantic City. Giant watermelon placed on end, carved into shape of crown, filled with fruit balls.	Changes calendar to current month.
5:45-6 PM FOOD	Food retrieved from refrigerator: baba ganoush, lavosh, salmon mousse, pita wedges, cruelty-free pâté.	Opens four bags of chips, two bags of pretzels, one container of French onion dip.

	Gay	*Straight*
6-6:15 PM **NAPKINS**	*Carefully folds matching cloth napkins into Bird of Paradise shapes.*	*Thinks of tearing off individual paper towels; decides to just put whole roll on coffee table*
6:15-6:30 PM **MUSIC**	*Vanessa Williams CD, rare Mary Ann Mobley recording, old Anita Bryant tape on reserve for sake of irony.*	*CCR, Grateful Dead, Led Zeppelin, ZZ Top, radio.*
6:30-6:45 PM **GUESTS ARRIVE**	*Guests bring potted plants, video of last party, fondue, Twister, treats for pet.*	*Two people bring more chips, three bring extra beer.*
6:45-7 PM **THE ICE**	*Unmolds ice cubes made from bottled water with mint leaves suspended in them; stores in silver aluminum ice bucket with matching tongs.*	*10 pound bag of nearly solid block of ice slowly melting in sink. Other guys vie for whose turn it is to hack at it.*
7-8 PM **PRE-PAGEANT/** **GAME**	*Discuss design ideas for backyard deck. Debate virtues of planting honeysuckle vs. wisteria.*	*Discuss type of wood planned for new deck. Offers made to come help build in coming weekends*

Gay   **Straight**

	Gay	**Straight**
EXTRA OUTDOOR LIGHT NEEDED	Japanese lanterns, citronella candles, yard torches, or string of lighted chili peppers.	Security light.
8-11 PM PAGEANT/GAME IN PROGRESS	Watch pageant from start to finish. Compare current host to Bert Parks; discuss who has tried the Toni Home Perm. Swear Miss Michigan forgot to take the wolverine off her head when she changed out of her state costume. Notice that Miss Iowa didn't get enough hairspray on her butt 'cause her suit is slipping. Realize that using Vaseline to brighten smile now gives it two uses. Play 'Spot the Silicone.' Cheer for girl with the snappiest response to question.	Get caught up in game, roaring, pounding floor, whistling, clapping. For some undisclosed reason, all are rooting for the same team, even though no one from that city. Amiable arguing over why team won or lost, who placed bets. Flipping reveals "Miss America" still in progress. Cheering resumes, consensus favoring the one with the biggest breasts, unconcerned whether they're real, implants, or spandex stretched over two football helmets.

HIS BACKYARD

Gay

"Goldie Hawn,"
"Samuel Goldwyn,"
"Whoopi Goldberg,"
"Jeff Goldblum,"
"Golda Meir"

uses every
third day

makes own
birdseed

Straight

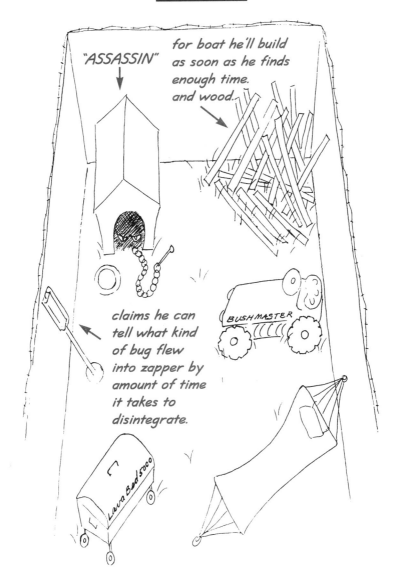

	Gay	Straight
11 PM PRIZES	Secret ballot taken among the guests. Host reveals results. Winner who had the best (cattiest) comments during the ceremony is voted Miss Congeniality and is awarded his own shoulder-to-hip satin sash and rhinestone tiara.	Host reveals winner of private pool who came closest to guessing winner and point spread. $22 in the pool, plus all the remaining beer—two cans
MIDNIGHT	Cleans up after everyone leaves.	Will clean up in the morning. Or afternoon.

Personality

Remember the old television program, "The Dating Game"? This is the part where you determine all the things you were supposed to learn about some lucky bachelor without seeing him or his surroundings. The inner man. You know, the one you think you'll have to remove surgically to examine.

General Qualities

	Gay	Straight
DOMINANT PHILOSOPHY	1. Have fun 2. Get laid	1. Get laid 2. Get ahead
NOTICES	Details	"The Big Picture"
CREATIVITY	Subtle changes or flourishes at every opportunity, for example, for a centerpiece to complement the Japanese meal, he'll use a collection of figurines, bonsai, a fan, and doll house furniture for a diorama depicting a geisha teahouse.	Someone mentions there's nothing in the center of the table—he adds the giant salt and pepper shakers from the stove.

Gay

GREATEST FANTASY

While shopping at a 95% off sale at Barneys, a producer approaches him, asking if he'd like the part of Hadrian's slave in a play to be staged in the newly restored Art Deco theater. He asks him to brunch with the co-star, Carol Channing, and guesses his age at 12 years less than he really is.

Having just finished giving the stewardess her first multiple orgasm, his best buddy, the pilot, is knocked out by a terrorist. He deals the infidel a wicked blow, while remaining clear-headed enough to be talked down from the tower. Unfortunately, the landing gear sticks, but he manages to release it with a plastic fork, when suddenly the wing catches fire, and the only thing handy to put it out. . .

WHILE MULLING OVER A PROBLEM, HE IDLY

adjusts hanging pictures to geometric perfection.

adjusts self.

OFFERS TO DRESS LIKE HE WANTS YOU TO

Gay

cheekbones,
cheekbones

faux

may try outfit
on when you're
not around

106
credit
cards

accessories

manages to slink

Straight

can't have too
much hair

faux

last full breath
45 minutes ago

tearaway
panties

not for
horses

can't walk,
only totters

not for
dusting

Gay **Straight**

	Gay	Straight
WHEN DEPRESSED HE	goes in debt from QVC orders, eats Ben & Jerry's straight from the carton, calls everyone he knows, starts smoking again, returns purchases mainly to argue with the clerks.	lies on bed fully dressed, stares at the ceiling.
WORST ENEMY	Windy day	IRS
ADAPTABILITY TO SETTING	Willingness, nay eagerness to change surroundings to suit him.	Ability to shut out shocking level of dirt, noise, inconvenience, if other factors met.
POLITICAL ACTIVITY	Attends marches, fund raisers, for specific causes like anti-discrimination, the environment, etc.	Heated arguments with supervisors, co-workers, your family, or you.

	Gay	Straight
FAVORITE HOLIDAYS	Halloween; Academy Awards night	New Year's Eve/Day; Superbowl Sunday
TO "GET AWAY FROM IT ALL" HE GOES TO THE NEAREST	mall.	national forest.

Conversational Style

DISCUSSING SELF	Talks about what he is.	Talks about what he does.
YOU TELL A JOKE	He laughs or giggles with enthusiasm, then squeezes your arm and cries, "You're too cold!"	He smiles briefly, then immediately responds with a story of his own.
HIS IDEA OF A JOKE	"Did you hear about the new Divorce Barbie? She comes with all of Ken's stuff."	"I finally found the perfect woman. She's 3 feet tall, has a flat head, and no teeth." Wait until there are only female witnesses before you kill him.
YOU TELL SOME JUICY GOSSIP	"No! You're kidding! Did you hear any more?" Doesn't really care if it's true or not; tells everyone.	"Who told you that?" Demands verification. Pretends he's not enjoying. Tells guys.

	Gay	
HE DESCRIBES THE MOVIE "THELMA AND LOUISE"	"Daring and original. A cross between 'Butch Cassidy' and 'Annie Get Your Gun.' I loved their sunglasses, and that turquoise convertible!"	"A chick flick."
YOU COMPLIMENT HIM ON A DISH HE HAS PREPARED.	"All you do is take six red potatoes, not those itty-bitty ones, the regular kind, 1/2 cup of milk—I only use skim—an onion, Vidalia, if possible, some freshly grated nutmeg and a little cilantro. Fifty minutes at 375° and there you are."	"Uh, well, my mom used to make something like it. I didn't have half the stuff, so I chopped up some leftover tacos."
YOU COMPLIMENT HIM ON SOMETHING HE'S WEARING	"Why thank you, it is wonderful, isn't it? Can you believe I found it at the bottom of the sale bin at Nordstrom's? I just hand wash it in lukewarm, then block it."	"Uh, thanks. My sister sent it for my birthday."

	Gay	Straight
YOU ASK HIM HOW YOUR NEW DRESS LOOKS	"I love it! Is it a Christian Lacroix? And in taffeta! You'll rival Bette Davis when she shocked society in 'Jezebel'!"	"Fine. Let's go."
YOU ASK HIM HOW YOUR MAKE-UP LOOKS	"Wise change of blush. That cerise really brings out your cheekbones."	"We're supposed to be there in five minutes."
YOU ASK HIM HOW HE LIKES YOUR NEW HAIRSTYLE	"That style is perfect for you! It reminds me of Joan Collins before the tragic fire on 'Dynasty.'"	"Why, did you cut it or something?"
YOU ASK HIM WHAT HIS FRIEND HAD TO SAY AFTER A 30-MINUTE PHONE CALL	Repeats both sides of entire conversation with additional commentary; takes 1 hour 15 minutes to re-tell.	"Nothing much."
FOLLOWING PHONE CALL, YOU ASK IF HIS FRIEND'S SISTER HAD HER BABY	"Yes, a little girl, named Kristina with a 'K' Gabriella, 8 pounds 3 ounces. I was thinking we should send a matinee jacket—I saw a darling one just the other day..."	"Forgot to ask."

HOW YOU LOOK TO HIM

Gay

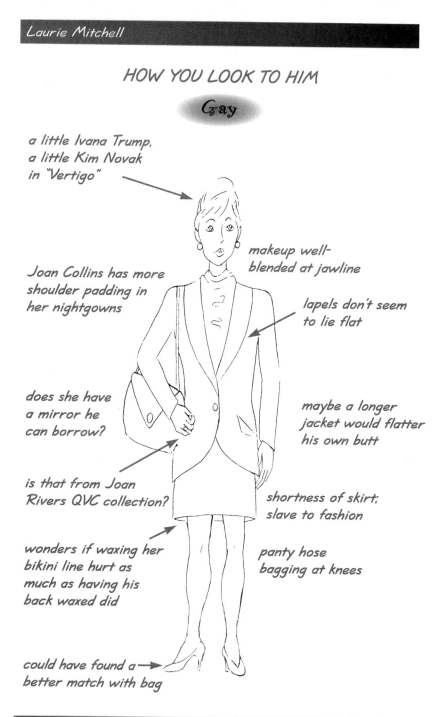

a little Ivana Trump,
a little Kim Novak
in "Vertigo"

makeup well-
blended at jawline

Joan Collins has more
shoulder padding in
her nightgowns

lapels don't seem
to lie flat

does she have
a mirror he
can borrow?

maybe a longer
jacket would flatter
his own butt

is that from Joan
Rivers QVC collection?

shortness of skirt;
slave to fashion

wonders if waxing her
bikini line hurt as
much as having his
back waxed did

panty hose
bagging at knees

could have found a
better match with bag

Straight

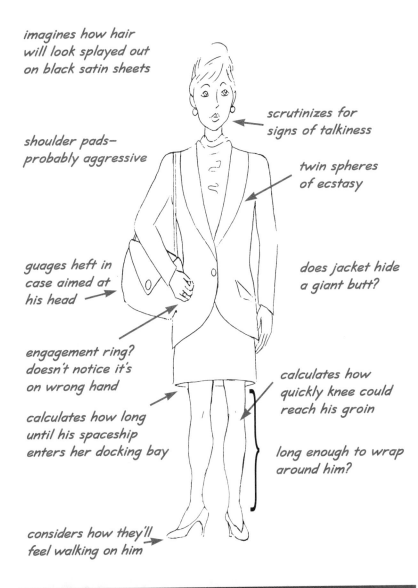

imagines how hair will look splayed out on black satin sheets

scrutinizes for signs of talkiness

shoulder pads— probably aggressive

twin spheres of ecstasy

guages heft in case aimed at his head

does jacket hide a giant butt?

engagement ring? doesn't notice it's on wrong hand

calculates how quickly knee could reach his groin

calculates how long until his spaceship enters her docking bay

long enough to wrap around him?

considers how they'll feel walking on him

	Gay	Straight
ASK HIM TO USE THE WORD 'CABINET' IN A SENTENCE	"All three of my china cabinets are simply stuffed."	"My rifle cabinet won't be big enough for the Howitzer I've got my eye on."

Ask Him to Complete the Following

	Gay	Straight
AL	Gore	Bundy
LAUREN	Bacall	Holly
STRIP	mall	tease
NAIL	file	gun or her
BEAT	egg whites until stiff peaks form.	the other guy at his own game
THE WORD 'UNCUT' SUGGESTS	uncircumcised.	an adult video.
WORDS AND EXPRESSIONS THE OTHER WILL NEVER, EVER USE	Adore. Fetching (adjective, not a verb involving a dog and a stick). Tacky. Fabulous. Divine. Could you please tell me where I might find...	Point spreads. Yo, Bubba! Fuckin' A. That really grinds my ass. Man, get a loada them warheads.

Relationships

	Gay	Straight
MOTHER	Very close, companionable, especially if he is comfortable with himself. May live very near her. May live with her.	Loves dearly, but she drives him crazy. Tries to please but feels it's never enough. Certain you'll eventually make him feel that way, too.
FATHER	Civil discussions when other family members present.	Never really agrees on anything, constantly arguing or agreeing to a truce for the holiday, but will go fishing with.
SISTER	Suspects her brother's true nature before anyone else. May result in a second bond in adult life.	He likes her a lot more than he admits, at least to her. Her boyfriend or husband is never good enough for her.

RESPONSE TO CHANGING SEASONS

Gay

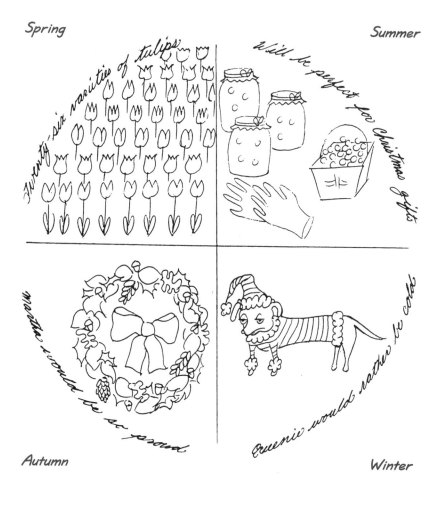

Spring

Summer

Autumn

Winter

Straight

Spring

Summer

Autumn

Winter

 **Gay**

Straight

	Gay	Straight
BROTHER	Doesn't speak of nearly as often as he does other family members. When he does, it's mostly in terms of career. Maintains a mutually respectful distance. Brother may also be his exact opposite, a real ramrod eagle scout.	Some long-standing combination of rivals and buddies. Unless his brother is gay.
FRIENDSHIPS WITH WOMEN	Great pals, extremely comfortable as there is no sexual tension. Usually forms a pact with a metabolically-challenged, smart-mouthed, sympathetic woman who has little luck with boyfriends and abysmal self-esteem.	World of women to whom he's not related broken into following categories: those to whom he is sexually attracted; those he finds sexually attractive but are off-limits, such as ex-girlfriends, ex-wives, bosses, etc.; and all the rest that he does not find sexually appealing, who to him are a curious third gender with whom he may be casual friends as long as they're not after the same job.

	Gay	Straight
FRIENDSHIPS WITH MEN	Seemingly endless number of unmarried men, 19 - 56 years old; propensity towards chattiness.	A few good friends, some married, some not, doesn't seem to matter. All within 5 years of his age.
MEETING YOUR FAMILY	Delighted to meet your mother. Spends most of his time with her, admiring house decor, garden, etc. Offers to help in kitchen, discusses whether it's necessary to make a roux for a smooth white sauce. Father is quiet, senses he wouldn't be interested in his gun collection. Sister indifferent; brother's lip curls.	Dreads meeting your mother. He is quieter and more polite than you've ever seen him, as he's struggling with memories of his own maternal misunderstandings. Father proudly shows him his gun collection. Sister jealous. Brother shakes hand firmly to establish himself as your protector.
YOU ASK HIM OVER FOR THANKSGIVING. HE	brings an aspic in an antique copper mold, tactfully disagrees with how the gravy is seasoned.	insists on carving the turkey. Sharpens knife for an inordinately long time.

YOU DON'T FEEL WELL. HIS RESPONSE

Straight

announces he left
toilet seat up in
case you need
to vomit.

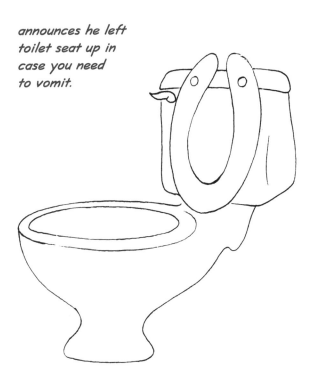

Gay Straight

	Gay	Straight
YOU ASK HIM TO HAND YOU THE MACE. HE LOOKS IN YOUR	spice cabinet.	purse.
AFTER DINNER	Helps clear table, rinses plates while flipping each one to check origin, stores leftovers into Tupperware, asks if you want them labeled.	In Barcalounger, asleep, mouth open, belt undone.

Cars

Although this would seem to belong in the Lifestyle section, it is not so much the type of car, as the critically different attitudes towards them.

	Gay	Straight
TO HIM, A CAR IS	one more accessory.	everything.
HIS RELATIONSHIP WITH HIS CAR CAN BEST BE DESCRIBED AS	love/hate.	love/lust.
TYPES OF CARS	Mini-jeep, mini-truck, VW Beetle, restored Woody, Saturns (guaranteed low maintenance), anything with detachable roof parts.	Corvette, van, jacked-up pickup, anything with body rust under continual repair _at his own hands_.

	Gay	Straight
TAKES HIS CAR IN TO HAVE	upholstery mended.	engine replaced.
DISCUSSING HIS NEW CAR	"My new car finally came. It took forever because I insisted on teal."	"I just drove my new XLZ5,000,000 off the lot today. Goes from 0 to 60 in two seconds. Fully loaded, turbo charged, 750 hp, with mag wheels. Best car since my old '69 Phallus. Talked the guy down from..."
INTERIOR OF CAR FEATURES A GARTER BELT HANGING FROM REARVIEW MIRROR	Can't explain it's origin, appears to be his size.	Swears it belonged to your predecessor, though price tag still on it.
NAMES HIS CAR	Flipper, Toto, Harley, Chitty-chitty bang-bang, The Beast.	The Roller, The Beemer, Gargantua, El Trucadero, The Heap.

FANTASY TRANSPORTATION

Gay

Straight

grateful
ex-virgin

The Hummer

	Gay	Straight
DRIVES HIS CAR	when he wants to go from one place to another.	whenever possible. Transportation is just an excuse; driving is an end in itself. Currently able to eat and speak on the phone while driving; if he could have sex and sleep while at the wheel, happiness would be complete.
PARKING	Will go up to 10 blocks out of his way to avoid parallel parking. In a parking lot, will take first thing he finds available to maximize time at destination.	Looks at tight or unusual parking spaces as an opportunity for personal challenge. Real sense of victory if he negotiates a space others passed up, even if he has to climb out the sunroof to exit car. Never a waste of time to circle 20 minutes for closest possible space, or park 1/2 mile away to avoid contact with another car. Will check for scratches immediately upon return.

Pop Culture Preferences

	Gay	*Straight*
FAVORITE MOVIES	*A Star is Born, Bringing up Baby, The Wizard of Oz, Gone with the Wind, Giant, Land of the Pharaohs, Outlaw, Some Like It Hot, Johnny Guitar, Sunset Boulevard, and Mommie Dearest.*	*The Terminator, The Magnificent Seven, The Dirty Dozen, The Great Escape, Die Hard, The Quiet Man, Top Gun, Bullitt, Cool Hand Luke, any 007 except for Casino Royale.*
FAVORITE WOODY ALLEN MOVIES	*Prefers everything after and including Annie Hall*	*Prefers everything before Annie Hall*
FAVORITE ACTRESSES - current	*Meryl Streep, Anjelica Huston, Shirley MacLaine, Glenn Close*	*Michelle Pfeiffer, Julia Roberts, Sharon Stone, Darryl Hannah*
FAVORITE ACTRESSES - vintage	*Bette Davis, Katherine Hepburn, Barbara Stanwyck, Marilyn Monroe, Jean Harlow.*	*Whoever's starring opposite Humphrey Bogart.*

	Gay	Straight
FAVORITE VILLAIN	Cruella de Ville	Dr. No
FAVORITE ACTORS - current	Brad Pitt, Antonio Banderas, Leonardo DiCaprio	Sylvester Stallone, Bruce Willis, Harrison Ford
FAVORITE ACTION/ ADVENTURE ACTOR WITH AN ACCENT	Mel Gibson	Sean Connery
FAVORITE GUY WHO STARS IN ACTION/ ADVENTURE MOVIES, WITH AN ACCENT	Jean-Claude Van Damme	Arnold Schwarzenegger
FAVORITE ACTORS - vintage	Cary Grant, Gregory Peck, William Powell, Montgomery Clift	Humphrey Bogart, James Cagney, John Wayne, Edward G. Robinson, Spencer Tracy

Reaction to Specific Movies

	Gay	Straight
STEEL MAGNOLIAS	Weeps openly, still sniffling during credits.	Disgusted. "She knew she shouldn't have a baby."

	Gay	**Straight**
ROOM WITH A VIEW	Rapt.	Bored, fidgety. Anxious for something, anything to happen.
DEER HUNTER	Leans forward during male bonding scenes.	Leans forward during Russian roulette scenes.
ROBOCOP	Covers eyes.	Mechanically eats popcorn, engrossed.
PRETTY WOMAN	Laughs merrily.	Drools.
SHOWGIRLS	Considers prime camp material. Invites 16-20 friends to midnight showing, laughs throughout.	Guiltily sneaks out to see, alone, in different part of town from where he lives.
FAVORITE TELEVISION SHOWS	The Gossip Show, Designing Women, Bewitched, Dynasty, Golden Girls, Absolutely Fabulous.	M*A*S*H, Seinfeld, 60 Minutes, American Gladiators.
FAVORITE TELEVISION SHOW TO WATCH IF THE SOUND IS BROKEN	Baywatch	Baywatch (pay attention to which gender is on screen when he breaks off in mid-sentence)

	Gay	*Straight*
FAVORITE FEMALE TELEVISION PERSONALTIES	Fran Drescher, Delta Burke, Roseanne	Jennifer Aniston, Pamela Lee, Heather Locklear
WHEN ANNA NICOLE SMITH APPEARS ON SCREEN HE	snickers.	gapes in wonder.
FAVORITE MALE TELEVISION PERSONALITIES	Scott Wolf, Dean Cain, Arthur Kent	John Goodman, Tim Allen, Mike Wallace
REVERED PBS ACTORS, formerly RSC, now immortalized on A&E	Jeremy Irons and Anthony Andrews	What?
FAVORITE STAR TREK CHARACTER	Captain James T. Kirk, years 1966-69	Worf
COMEDIANS	Lily Tomlin, Sandra Bernhard	Robin Williams, Gallagher
FAVORITE "SATURDAY NIGHT LIVE" MIKE MYERS CHARACTER	Linda Richman	Wayne
FAVORITE "SNL" DANA CARVEY CHARACTER	Church Lady	Garth

THE WORD "TROPHY" SUGGESTS

Gay

OR

Straight

OR

	Gay	Straight
FAVORITE CLASSIC "SNL" CHARACTER	Gilda Radner's Roseanne Roseannadanna	John Belushi's Samurai warrior
TELEVISED SPORTS	The Olympics	Football, baseball, basketball, golf – basically anything with a ball in it.
FAVORITE ATHLETES TO WATCH	Pete Sampras, Brian Boitano, Phillipe Candelero, Alberto Tomba (that Italian skier), most pitchers and first basemen	Michael Jordan, Charles Barkley, Wayne Gretsky, Joe Montana, George Foreman
GENERAL CELEBRITIES	Bette Midler, Joan Rivers, Elizabeth Taylor, John F. Kennedy, Jr., Oprah, Miss Manners, Zsa Zsa Gabor, Liza Minnelli, and, of course, her mother	Bill Gates, Norman Schwartzkoff, Kathy Ireland, Larry King, Rush Limbaugh, Hugh Hefner, G. Gordon Liddy, Howard Stern, Lee Iaccoca, Frederique
FAVORITE SAINTS	Saint Sebastian	Saint Louis Cardinals

YOU ASK HIS OPINION OF SKATER'S 'MUFF'

Gay

"isn't it great?
do you think it's
winter mink or
sable?"

Straight

"can't tell yet.
wait'll she
spins again".

Musical / Artistic Preferences

Gay

	Gay	Straight
COUNTRY	Tammy Wynette	Hank Williams, Jr.
CLASSICAL	Chopin	Beethoven
OPERA	Madame Butterfly	Tommy
POP, STILL PERFORMING	Diana Ross, Cher, Barbra Streisand, Johnny Mathis	Everybody else
AUTHORS	E. M. Forster, Anne Rice, Oscar Wilde, Evelyn Waugh, A. A. Milne, Jackie Collins	John Grisham, Louis L'Amour, Tom Clancy, Jack London
FAVORITE 20TH CENTURY AMERICAN AUTHOR FORCED TO READ IN HIGH SCHOOL	William Faulkner	Ernest Hemingway
POETRY	Walt Whitman, W. H. Auden	Muhammad Ali, Dr. Suess
ART	Michelangelo, Caravaggio (big giveaway), Nagel	M. C. Escher, those 3-D pictures, old album covers
PHOTOGRAPHY	Herb Ritts	"Sports Illustrated" Swimsuit Calendar

Consensually Private Meeting
Outside of Usual Context
(It's a little too early to call it a date.)

 Gay **Straight**

	Gay	Straight
MANNERS	Pulls your chair out for you, with a flourish	Pulls your chair out awkwardly, shyly, or lets the waiter do it.
EYE CONTACT	Looks you in the eye (has nothing to fear), unless you're wearing terrific shoes, or there's a cute guy standing behind you.	Glances in your eyes as if touching base; meanwhile visually roams the room, taking in the waitress, your hair, the clock, his watch, the check, his napkin, your breasts, his drink, your lips, your unfinished piece of pie. . .
CAN'T FIND A PEN TO SIGN THE CHECK. YOU OFFER YOUR EYEBROW PENCIL. HE	happily accepts.	would rather use his own blood.

	Gay	Straight
TOUCHING	May touch you in a friendly, non-suggestive way, especially after sharing a delicious piece of gossip.	Won't touch you, unless briefly on elbow or back when escorting through a door. Real touching is reserved for before, during, and possibly after, sex.
VISITING HIS APARTMENT FOR THE FIRST TIME	Proudly shows off his petit-point; relaxed, as if all third dates start this way.	Proudly shows off his CD/laserdisc collection. Hopes it will impart the insights into his character that he's too uncomfortable to express.
FIXES YOU	Hot amaretto-flavored cocoa	a Harvey-wallbanger
YOU RELATE A TRAUMATIC CHILDHOOD INCIDENT THAT EXPLAINS CURRENT BEHAVIOR. IN RESPONSE HE	says, "I know just how you feel. When I was eight my babysitter. . ."	kisses you lightly on nose, musses your hair. Smiles, says, "Do you always analyze everything so much?"

	Gay	Straight
ASKS	"Do you want to watch a movie? I have "South Pacific" on tape and I can make some popcorn."	"Do you want to go to bed?"
FOREPLAY	You initiate	He initiates
SEX	If you actually get him to the bed, says: a. "I'm really into just cuddling, aren't you?" b. "Let's concentrate on <u>you</u> tonight."	Two rules: a. There's no such thing as too much. b. There's probably no such thing as enough.

CELEBRATES YOUR BIRTHDAY

 Gay

Straight

TAKES YOU OUT TO

your favorite restaurant

his favorite restaurant

DANCES AROUND

the floor

the topic of commitment

SURPRISES YOU WITH COLORED, RUBBER

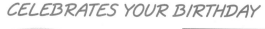

balloons

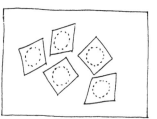

condoms

Gay

 Straight

PRESENTS YOU WITH A

teddy

teddy

RENTS

videos

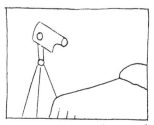

camcorder and tripod

DIMS THE LIGHTS TO BETTER APPRECIATE

the movie

his new glow-in-
the-dark accessories

A Few Final Pointers

General Giveaways

THESE TELL-TALE SIGNS PRETTY NEARLY ALWAYS MEAN THAT HE'S GAY.

1. Theme parties. A party without a premise is just a gathering, and that happens every Sunday afternoon. Reasons to decorate, celebrate, make this party distinguishable from the many others. Watch for festivities surrounding things like Hawaiian luaus and Faye Dunaway's Birthday and Film Festival. "Getting together for the Big Game" doesn't count.

2. No matter how much taller you are than he is, or by how much you outweigh him, he is still willing to dance with you.

3. Knows anything at all about any soap opera. Doesn't count if he's been in traction six months from a Harley accident.

4. Mentions 'having tea,' a 'tea party,' or 'tea dances,' and he's about as British as Doris Day.

5. Holds opinions on moisturizers. Asks your preference, or gives you tips on selecting one.

6. Uses words like 'rococo' even though he never had an art class, never been a carpenter.

7. Kitsch. Not the occasional lime-green toilet seat cover that merely indicates a lapse in taste. Really valuing, pur-

chasing, and proudly displaying items such as glitter-covered glass grapes, Tammy Faye Bakker dolls, pink flamingoes, and supermarket tabloids. Expect to be invited to a Velveeta cheese luncheon or a white trash dinner followed by a show-ing of "Valley of the Dolls."

General Giveaways

A FEW HELPFUL CLUES IN HOMING IN ON THE STRAIGHT, SINGLE ONES STILL OUT THERE.

1. Watches professional wrestling, doesn't laugh.

2. Lets <u>you</u> trim his hair, moustache, or beard.

3. Avid comic book reader or collector. (I have no idea why, but there you are.)

4. Spiders, scorpions, reptiles, or amphibians kept as pets.

5. Hockey fan. (May not apply in Canada.)

6. Pot-belly. Just doesn't happen, or a gay man will dress to disguise.

Don't be fooled by the following characteristics into thinking he's necessarily gay:

EXCESSIVE NEATNESS
Just because he's anal-retentive doesn't mean he's gay. Fussiness, however, may not make him desirable in either case.

WONDERFUL ART OR ANTIQUES COLLECTION
It can happen. If you find that it's strictly for investment purposes, you've got a straight one—aesthetically bankrupt perhaps—but a straight one with a lot of money.

LACK OF MANY WOMEN IN HIS PAST
There's still a few shy ones left. Besides, does few men in your life make you a lesbian?

HE'S WEARING A PIERCED EARRING
It's clip-ons you want to watch out for. If he has multiple pierced earrings, he may still be in that grunge/punk/I-want-to-look-irritating pose, but also consider that he may not have stopped with his ears. . .

SENSITIVE NATURE, EXPRESSES FEELINGS
There really are some straight men who feel what you do. Really.

Conversely, don't assume these seemingly irrefutable indicators prove that he's straight:

"PLAYBOY" MAGAZINE IN HIS APARTMENT

Some people really <u>do</u> buy it for the interviews, and there's a certain kitsch / collector appeal in a nude Miss America or President's daughter.

CREW CUT, FLANNEL SHIRT, DUNGAREES, HOBNAIL BOOTS

It's a matter of carefulness v. casualness. Look for clothes that are not new but show no signs of wear, and a rather smooth or carefully groomed face that doesn't match the seeming ruggedness of the outfit.

EX-MARINE

No better way out of Kansas.

HAS AN EX-WIFE, AND CHILDREN THAT LOOK A LOT LIKE HIM

<u>Never</u> assume this proves anything.

PROPOSES MARRIAGE

If his family is very conservative or wealthy (all of their paintings are portraits, he's the only boy and there's a Roman numeral after his name), he may be under more pressure to find a wife. His friends will refer to you as his "beard." Lovely.

LAMENTS THE DEMISE OF TRADITIONAL FEMININITY

Gays miss the feminine ideal as much as straight men do, though the reasons may be more aesthetic than personal.

CLIP AND SAVE

This is a sampling of other women's brief checklists, should you not yet have this book memorized. Besides, it's hard to find the exact reference while hiding it behind your menu.

1. Barbra Streisand. Has more than one album, admires her, ever mentions her name. That's about it.

2. Reads "GQ"; has a cute name like Toby or Kenny.

3. Dresses neatly; very nice manners.

4. Owns a can of Lysol, appears to use it.

5. He really enjoyed being a waiter.

6. Notices—and knows names of—your house-plants.

7. "At this age (42), I assume every single man is gay until he proves otherwise."

HIS HOUSEPLANTS

Gay

needs 4 hours inside, 3 hours outside, 2 hours indirect light, 15 hours complete darkness— gets it.

requires constant misting—currently in an antique umbrella stand.

takes 1 teaspoon Evian every 3 days—no more, no less.

cannot stand more than a 4° temperature change, blooms once a year at midnight— friends come over to watch.

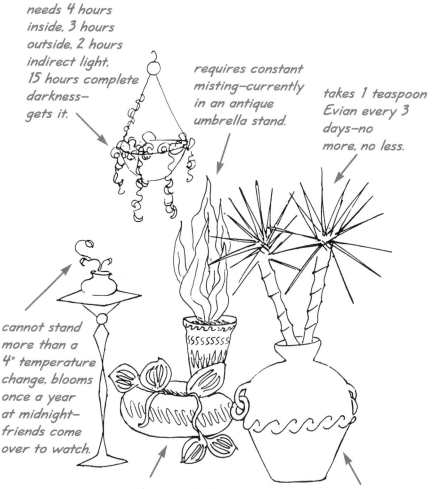

selected plant to match upholstery.

carried urn back from Mykonos— won't believe it's identical to Pier 1's.

Straight

mildew

QUIZ - See how much you've learned

1. Your Purse
A. Regards your purse resentfully as an unbroachable, mysterious container, bulging with feminine devices that you would gladly share with every woman on the planet, but keep secret from him.
B. Compliments you on your ability to accessorize, asks if it's a Versace.

2. Pupils dilate
A. during the fifteenth round of the heavyweight title bout.
B. as the Tony Award for Best Musical is announced.

3. You admire a piece of his wooden furniture. He says it came from
A. a local antiques mall that he frequents each weekend in search of a complete set of Paramount lobby cards.
B. his fully equipped workshop, made from a tree he felled himself.

4. While out walking together you encounter a street brawl. He
A. pushes you in a doorway while he breaks it up / joins in.
B. joins you in the doorway.

5. While taking a sunny lunch break together you pass a shirtless construction worker using a jackhammer. Your companion says,
A. "Man, I could really use one of those to bust up my old driveway."

B. "Gosh, I hope he's wearing at least a sun factor 15."

6. You mention your Junior year abroad. He surprises you with his
A. amazing knowledge of the British Royal Family.
B. disturbing admiration of the rise of the Third Reich.

7. To him, 'Calvin' is
A. a fabulous designer with great ads.
B. Hobbes' best friend.

8. Changes topic abruptly when
A. you bring up subject of marriage and children.
B. you bring up subject of marriage and children.

9. Upon suggesting a trip to the South, he is
A. thrilled, since the South is the home of antebellum mansions, darling accents, debutante balls, mint juleps, Mardi Gras, and bread pudding.
B. appalled, since the South is the source of inbred, scary rednecks à la "Deliverance," grits, hot, sticky weather, and Bible Belt alligator wrestlers.

10. While on a peaceful country drive you come across road kill that appears to have been a human male. In an effort to determine whether it was straight or gay, you find
A. $7.83 in pocket change.
B. Hand lotion.

Answers to Quiz

1.A, 2.A, 3.B, 4.A, 5.A, 6.B, 7.B, 8.A or B (bonus) 9.B, 10.A
He probably admires Kevin Johnson.

1.B, 2.B, 3.A, 4.B, 5.B, 6.A, 7.A, 8.A or B, 9.A, 10.B.
He probably admires RuPaul.

If 70% of the answers fall in the 'gay' category, but he still swears he loves you, wants to marry you, father your children, _and_ is an eager bed-bouncer, you may be one of the few lucky ones who finds a friend and companion who won't abandon you during the NBA playoffs.

If 70% of the answers fall in the 'straight' category, _and_ he is virulent and vocal in his opposition to gays, he may be trying to hide his suspected/feared true nature from others, you, and himself. Or, he may just be a jerk.

Reminder: Men, both straight and gay, come in all shapes, sizes, races, and ages. You need to learn not only what you think you're seeing, but what he's trying to tell you, or hide from you, as well. Good luck.